Your Guide to Government

What are the levels of government?

Baron Bedesky

Crabtree Publishing Company
www.crabtreebooks.com

Crabtree Publishing Company

www.crabtreebooks.com

Author: Baron Bedesky
Coordinating editor: Chester Fisher
Series and project editor: Scholastic Ventures
Project manager: Kavita Lad (Q2AMEDIA)
Art direction: Dibakar Acharjee (Q2AMEDIA)
Cover design: Ranjan Singh (Q2AMEDIA)
Design: Ruchi Sharma (Q2AMEDIA)
Photo research: Sakshi Saluja (Q2AMEDIA)
Editor: Molly Aloian
Proofreader: Crystal Sikkens
Project editor: Robert Walker
Production coordinator: Katherine Kantor
Font management: Mike Golka
Prepress technician: Ken Wright

Photographs:
Cover: R. Gino Santa Maria/Shutterstock, J. Helgason/
Shutterstock (background); Title page: David L.
Moore-Hawaii/Alamy; P4: Anyka/Shutterstock;
P5: Emin Kuliyev/Shutterstock; P6: Stephen Coburn/
Shutterstock; P7: Tech. Sgt. William Greer/U.S. Air
Force/DOD Media; P8: Jay Laprete/Associated Press;
P9: Thinkstock Images/Jupiter Images; P10: David R.
Frazier Photolibrary, Inc./Alamy; P11: Rich Legg/
Istockphoto; P12: Bebeto Matthews/Associated Press;
P13: Vadim Kozlovsky/Shutterstock; P14: David R.
Frazier Photolibrary, Inc./Alamy; P15: Donald R.
Swartz/Shutterstock; P16: NearTheCoast.com/
Alamy; P17: Nyul/Dreamstime; P18: Nick Ut/
Associated Press; P19: Mike Norton/Dreamstime;
P20: Ziggymaj/Istockphoto; P21: Colin & Linda
McKie/Shutterstock; P22: Jgroup/BigStockPhoto;
P23: HO/Associated Press; P24: Charles Dharapak/
Associated Press; P25: Ieva Geneviciene/Shutterstock;
P26: Yuri Arcurs/Shutterstock; P27: Chris Schmidt/
Istockphoto; P28: Patrick Frilet/Rex Features; P29:
Positive image/Alamy; P30: The Desktop Studio/
Istockphoto; P31: Denise Kappa/Shutterstock

Library and Archives Canada Cataloguing in Publication

Bedesky, Baron
    What are the levels of government? / Baron Bedesky.

(Your guide to government)
Includes index.
ISBN 978-0-7787-4327-9 (bound).--ISBN 978-0-7787-4332-3 (pbk.)

    1. United States--Politics and government--Juvenile literature.
I. Title. II. Series.

JK40.B43 2008   j320.473   C2008-903657-3

Library of Congress Cataloging-in-Publication Data

Bedesky, Baron.
    What are the levels of government? / Baron Bedesky.
        p. cm. -- (Your guide to government)
    Includes index.
    ISBN-13: 978-0-7787-4332-3 (pbk. : alk. paper)
    ISBN-10: 0-7787-4332-2 (pbk. : alk. paper)
    ISBN-13: 978-0-7787-4327-9 (reinforced library binding : alk. paper)
    ISBN-10: 0-7787-4327-6 (reinforced library binding : alk. paper)
    1. United States--Politics and government--Juvenile literature. I. Title.
II. Series.

JK40.B43 2008
320.473--dc22
                                                          2008025379

Crabtree Publishing Company

www.crabtreebooks.com   1-800-387-7650

Published in Canada
Crabtree Publishing
616 Welland Ave.
St. Catharines, ON
L2M 5V6

Published in the United States
Crabtree Publishing
PMB16A
350 Fifth Ave., Suite 3308
New York, NY 10118

Published in the United Kingdom
Crabtree Publishing
White Cross Mills
High Town, Lancaster
LA1 4XS

Published in Australia
Crabtree Publishing
386 Mt. Alexander Rd.
Ascot Vale (Melbourne)
VIC 3032

Contents

The Government

In the United States, teams of people run our cities, states, and the country. We call these teams government. We elect people to be part of the government. They make rules we must obey. They also protect and help us.

Local government teams work in your community. These local governments run schools, police stations, and fire stations. They also run hospitals, city buses, libraries, and parks. The **state government** manages important projects for the whole state such as building roads and bridges. The **federal government** works on projects that the whole country needs. For example, it prints our money and delivers our mail.

The government controls what we ship and what is shipped to our country.

Imagine if the government did not control things like streets and traffic!

How do you take care of the 300 million people that live in the U.S.? It takes a lot of work! It takes many different governments to handle such a big job. Government is everywhere because people are everywhere.

Levels of Government

There are levels of government. Each level of government has its own responsibilities. Every level makes sure not to do the work of another level. All levels must communicate with each other.

Local government handles many smaller projects in the community. This may be something simple such as fixing a sidewalk or cutting the grass in the park. They complete larger projects as well, such as picking up the trash for a whole city every week.

Local governments build libraries where people can study or borrow books.

The federal government uses these soldiers to keep the entire country safe.

State government makes many **laws**, especially laws against crime. It also makes laws for schools and families. These laws treat everyone who lives in the state equally. The federal government also makes laws and decides how to spend our tax money. It runs the military, which keeps us safe.

FACT BOX

Our country has one federal government and 50 different state governments. It also has close to 90,000 smaller local governments.

Different Rules

Local governments look at only the people and problems in a small area. A town may want to make people stop their cars on a busy corner.

Imagine a flood damaging land in a large section of a state. This problem is too big for one city to handle. But it only happened in one state.

That state's government makes and follows rules for helping the flood victims.

Local leaders make decisions for local issues, like where businesses can open. Here leaders cut a ribbon to open a new business.

The federal government makes decisions for national problems. The federal government made laws to make all airports in the U.S. safe.

The federal government does not make local or state decisions. This government makes rules that everyone in the entire country follows. These laws are the same for each person, in every part of the country.

School Governments

States also have many school **districts**. The word district describes an area or community. A school district is an area of schools. There may be a few public schools in your area. They belong to the same school district. A large city might have many school districts.

Each school district in the U.S. has a government. We have more than 16,000 school district governments in our country. School boards make the decisions for the schools and students in school districts. School boards have a leader called a superintendent.

One school district contains the elementary, junior high, and high schools in an area.

MIDDLETON HEIGHTS ELEMENTARY

The school board hires teachers and decides which textbooks to use.

Each school district takes care of its own schools. They decide what to do for the students, teachers, buildings, and buses. Some schools may need more space. Others may need library books or more teachers. A school board will try to give each school what it needs.

11

City Governments

The United States has about 19,000 large cities. Living in a city can be very different from living in a small town or on a farm. The people in a city have special needs because everything is so close together.

A city government will help people get from place to place by setting up a bus system or a subway. It makes sure the fire department has the correct equipment to deal with emergencies in tall buildings. A city government has to hire many workers. They take care of a large number of people living in the city.

The leaders of this city government talk about what will be good for people living in the city.

Many city governments hire people like garbage collectors to keep the city clean and safe.

Each city has a leader called a mayor. The mayor gets help from the people in his government. Different people in the government are in charge of different projects. For example, one person can be in charge of police. Another person will be in charge of all the parks.

District Governments

No single government can give people everything they need. That is why we have many district governments for special jobs. Sometimes they have names such as **boards** or **commissions**. The people in these governments are experts in one subject. The U.S. has more than 28,000 special district governments.

Special district governments usually work on one project. The project may be making sure everyone has clean water to drink. It could also be a government for all of the libraries in one area.

A special government controls the buses and trains like this one in Chicago. This job was too big for the city government to handle.

This is the Brooklyn Bridge in New York City. The Port Authority makes sure the bridges, tunnels, and airports in New York and New Jersey are safe.

The Chicago Transit Authority runs all the buses and trains in that city. The Port Authority of New York and New Jersey runs all the seaports around New York City. It also takes care of all of the bridges, tunnels, and airports. These are both examples of special districts.

FACT BOX

The Port Authority of New York and New Jersey has its own police force with 1,600 members.

County Governments

Every state has **counties**. You will find more than 3,000 counties in the United States. A small state like Delaware has only three counties. A large state like Texas has 254 counties. Counties can be large or small. Whether people live in a city, in the country, or somewhere in between, everyone lives in a county.

Nearly all counties have their own governments. We might call the government a board of supervisors, a county commission, or a county council. A county mayor or a county manager leads the county government. The county government meets in a place called the **county seat**.

These leaders work for the county government. The county government serves people in cities, towns, and everywhere in between inside one county.

County governments might build parks for everyone in a county to enjoy.

A county government is usually different from a city government. A county government cares for people who do not live in cities, as well as those who do.

County governments will use their own sheriff, courts, and jails. This protects people who live in areas where there is no police force.

State Governments

Each of the 50 states has its own government. Almost every state government has two groups of people. We call one group the **Senate**. Most states call the other group the **House of Representatives**. Some states also call it an Assembly. Each state government works in that state's capital city.

Every state government has a leader called a **governor**. The governor also chooses many of the people who work in the government. They help decide how a state will spend its money.

Governor Schwarzenegger leads the people of California.

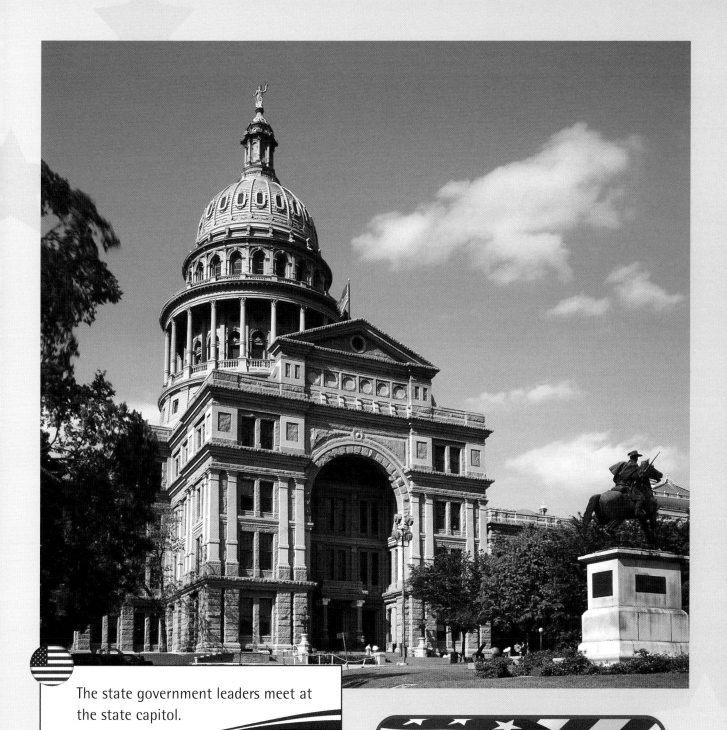

The state government leaders meet at the state capitol.

Each state government has much power and can create its own laws for the people who live there. So people in Iowa can have different laws than people in New York. State laws cannot go against the laws of the federal government, however.

FACT BOX

Governor Arnold Schwarzenegger of California was a famous bodybuilder. He has also starred in over 30 movies.

The State's Jobs

State governments can make their own decisions. These decisions depend on the needs of the people in that state.

Every state has different needs. Some large states need more highways because of their very large size. Other states located in dry and hot areas must have plans on how to share water. States with many large cities will have different laws than those with much farmland. State governments will help form different local governments to help with its special needs.

There are 50 states, so there are 50 state governments.

Each state takes care of its own needs, like building highways.

States like Texas and Florida sometimes have hurricanes. The state governments there must have plans for these kinds of disasters. The government in the state of Kansas, for example, does not make laws in case of hurricanes. They have other types of problems instead. Each state decides what the people living there need. States like Washington and Oregon have many forests. Those state governments have passed laws protecting the trees. States with fewer forests do not need these laws.

Federal Government

Nearly every government, including the federal government, has three branches. The **legislative branch** makes the laws. The **executive branch** makes sure people obey the laws. The **judicial branch** includes all the courts. The courts decide what to do when people break laws.

The president of the United States leads the country. He also leads the executive branch of the government. **Congress** runs the legislative branch. The United States Supreme Court leads the judicial branch. All three branches are separate from each other. Yet all three must work together to get things done.

The president lives and works in the White House.

These people listen to cases in the most important court in the country.

Most people in the federal government work in Washington, D.C. It is our capital city. D.C. stands for District of Columbia. It is unusual because it does not belong to any state.

FACT BOX

New York City was the first capital city of our country. Philadelphia became the next capital city before the government picked Washington D.C. in 1800.

Federal Jobs

The federal government makes decisions that affect the whole country. It leads our military. This includes the Army, Navy, Air Force, Marines, and the Coast Guard.

The federal government deals with the governments of all other countries. It can make agreements to act peacefully or to protect each other in wars. The federal government also arranges for buying and selling goods such as oil, food, cars, computers, and clothes, with other countries.

The president is in charge of all the military.

The federal government makes our money. Coins and bills are the same in all 50 states.

The federal government makes all the money we use every day. Can you imagine if all 50 states in our country used different money? People who travel to many different states would get confused. They could not use money from one state until they visited that state again.

The federal government collects much of our taxes, which is the money people pay for the government. Then the federal government decides how to use this money.

Government Money

You may wonder how the government pays for everything it does. Most of its money comes from taxes. Different governments collect tax money from everyone.

Local and district governments collect taxes for their own projects. School districts might get their taxes from people who own homes. The more expensive the home, the more taxes people must pay.

Cities and counties get tax money, too. Most get their taxes when people shop. Taxes are added to the price of the items people buy. States and counties get money the same way.

Taxes may be added to the price of what we buy.

People pay taxes from the money they make while they work.

The state and federal governments collect other taxes. They take taxes from people's paychecks. They can tax companies who want to do business. They tax people and companies for the things they own.

All of these taxes pay for everything the governments do.

FACT BOX

If someone earns $3.00, he or she pays about $1.00 in taxes. So instead of bringing home $3.00, he or she keeps $2.00.

Native Americans

Before the United States was a country, Native Americans lived here. When settlers moved in, there were disagreements with Native Americans about who owned the land. Sometimes there was fighting between both sides. The government also fought with the Native Americans.

By 1851, the federal government started to set up large **reservations**. No settlers moved in to these pieces of land. The government wanted the Native Americans to live there. Today, about 300 different reservations exist in the United States. Some reservations have more land than the state of Rhode Island!

Native Americans lived in the U.S. long before it was a country.

Native American governments own businesses like the Hard Rock Café.

Native people have formed their own governments on the reservations. They call these special governments tribal councils. The councils look after their people. Many collect taxes for their own people. These taxes pay for the special needs of the Native Americans.

FACT BOX

The United States has more than 550 different tribal governments.

Seeing Governments

The next time you see a police officer or fire fighter, you will know they work for the government. You may see people repairing a road or throwing trash into a garbage truck. Do you see all the signs on the street? Our government put them there for all of us to use. These examples show what the government can do for us.

Almost every person in our country uses a service offered by a government every day. For children, schools remain the most important example of a service. Someone in a government helps decide what you should learn. If you eat a school lunch, the federal government helped pay for it.

The government helps schools choose healthy foods to serve students.

Police officers are government employees.

We need different levels of government. They divide many projects between them. One government cannot give people everything they need. Instead, different governments share the work. This makes it easier to give people the services they need most.

Glossary

board An organized group representing a project or business

commission An organized group allowed to perform specific duties

Congress The combination of the Senate and House of Representatives

county An area within a state with its own local government

county seat The city or town where the county government holds meetings

district A region within a city, county, or state run by local government

executive branch The group within a government that makes sure laws are obeyed

federal government The government group in charge of the whole country

governor The elected leader of any state government

House of Representatives The larger lower branch of a federal or state government

judicial branch The group within a government that makes decisions in court

law A rule made by the government

legislative branch The group within a government that makes laws

local government A group of people in charge of a community

reservation An area of land set aside for Native Americans

Senate The upper branch of a federal or state government

state government The government group in charge of a whole state

Index

Printed in the U.S.A.